Cats

by Diana Noonan

Cover ©Harcourt Index; 3–4 ©Photolibrary.com; 5 ©Alamy; 6 ©Image After; 7 ©Telescope; 8 ©Lucy Best; 9–10 ©Alamy; 11–13 ©Photolibrary.com; 14 ©Harcourt Index.

Printed in Mexico

ISBN 10: 0-15-350400-5
ISBN 13: 978-0-15-350400-6

Ordering Option
ISBN 10: 0-15-350332-7 (Grade 2 Below-Level Collection)
ISBN 13: 978-0-15-350332-0 (Grade 2 Below-Level Collection)
ISBN 10: 0-15-357427-5 (package of 5)
ISBN 13: 978-0-15-357427-6 (package of 5)

2 3 4 5 6 7 8 9 10 050 15 14 13 12 11 10 09 08 07

What Is My Cat's Name?

My cat's name is Sugar.
She is sweet like sugar.
Sometimes she rides in
my bicycle basket.

What Are Cats?

Cats are mammals.
Mother mammals make
milk for their babies.
Baby cats are called kittens.

Where Does My Cat Live?

My cat lives in our house. She sleeps in a special basket.

Sometimes my cat sleeps on my bed.

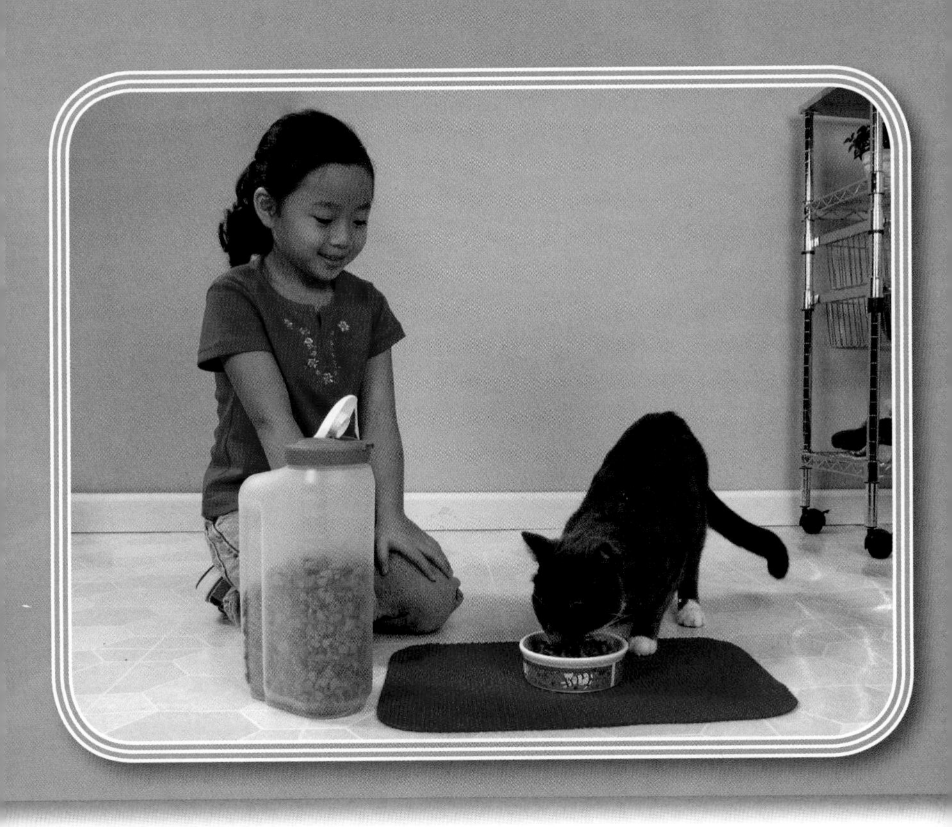

What Does My Cat Eat?

Some cats eat canned cat food.
My cat eats dry cat food.

Cats drink lots of water. Milk is not good for cats to drink.

What Do Cats Do?

Some cats use cat doors to go in and out.

Some cats use scratching posts to sharpen their claws.

What Do I Do with My Cat?

I hold my cat every day.

I play with my cat.
She gets exercise chasing things.

My cat sits with me when
I am reading.

I love my cat.
My cat loves me.

Think Critically

1. What facts did you learn about all cats when you read this book?
2. What do some cats use to sharpen their claws?
3. What are some things that cat owners can do with their cats?
4. What is something that people can do to make it easy for their cat to go in and out?
5. The cat in this book is called Sugar because she is sweet like sugar. If you had a cat, what would you name it and why?

Science

Make a Fact List Make a fact list about cats. Draw a picture of your favorite type of cat.

School-Home Connection Tell a family member what you learned when you read *Cats*. Talk about how big cats (lions, tigers, leopards) are alike and different from small cats.

Word Count: 158